ELEMENTS OF 18TH CENTURY COUNTERPOINT

WILLIAM G. ANDREWS
MOLLY SCLATER

GORDON V. THOMPSON MUSIC

A Division of Warner/Chappell Music Canada Ltd.
85 Scarsdale Road, Don Mills, Ontario M3B 2R2
Printed in Canada

WILLIAM G. ANDREWS graduated from the Royal Conservatory of Music in Piano and Voice and from the Faculty of Music, University of Toronto. His post graduate work was in Paris and Nice where he studied with Mme Aline van Barentzen on a French government scholarship. He also attended Master Classes at the Mozarteum in Salzburg, Austria and the Banff School of Fine Arts in Alberta, Canada.

Mr. Andrews is a member of the Theory Faculty of the Royal Conservatory of Music, where he serves as a lecturer and examiner in Harmony, Counterpoint, Analysis, History and Musicianship. He also lectures at the Faculty of Music, University of Toronto and the Summer School of the Royal Conservatory of Music. He is one of the Architects of the current Harmony, Counterpoint, Analysis, History, Keyboard Harmony, Musicianship and Ear-Training programmes at the Royal Conservatory of Music and has given numerous workshops on these subjects across Canada, and Internationally.

MOLLY SCLATER was born in Edinburgh, Scotland, where she received her early education. She graduated from Branksome Hall and continued her studies at the Royal Conservatory of Music. She holds a Bachelor of Music degree from the University of Toronto, an Associate Diploma from the Royal Conservatory of Music in Singing (A.T.C.M.) and an Associate Diploma from the Royal Canadian College of Organists (A.R.C.C.O.).

Miss Sclater has been a member of the Theory and Ear-Training Faculty of the Royal Conservatory of Music for many years as well as a member of their Board of Examiners (Theory) and Theory Committee. She has served several terms as Chairman of the Curriculum, Examinations & Syllabus Committee and has lectured at the Royal Conservatory of Music Summer School.

Molly Sclater was appointed Theory Co-ordinator in 1980 and is one of the Architects of the Complete Theory Programme of the Royal Conservatory of Music.

In addition to these activities, Miss Sclater has served as Organist and Choir Director at several Toronto churches and has conducted Theory workshops from coast to coast in Canada.

Thompson publications by these authors

Keys to Sight Reading and Musicianship
Molly Sclater, Boyanna Toyich, Wm. Andrews, Joe Ringhofer
Books 1 to 6 — contain progressively difficult Baroque and Classical pieces. Useful in early piano grades and the forms required for grade 3 harmony.
Book 7 — contains imitation, canons and fugues. Useful for grade 4 harmony

Book 8 — contains sonatinas, including sonata form and rondo. Useful for more advanced piano grades and the forms required for grade 4 harmony.

Keys to Music Analysis and Melody Writing
Molly Sclater, Kathryn Sinclair, William Andrews
Books 1 to 5
For grades 3, 4, 5 Harmony, Grade 4 Counterpoint & Grade 5 Analysis

Introduction to Materials of Western Music
Molly Sclater, William Andrews
For Grade 3 Harmony

Keys to Music History, Vol. I
William Andrews, Joe Ringhofer

Materials of Western Music — Vols. 1-2-3
William Andrews, Molly Sclater

Keys to Music Rudiments
Molly Sclater, Kathryn Sinclair, Boris Berlin
6 workbooks and a textbook covering Preliminary, Grade 1 and Grade 2 Rudiments

Keys to Music Rudiments — Answers and Approaches
Molly Sclater, Joe Ringhofer

Harmony — A Summary of Techniques of Western Music
William Andrews

48 Fugues of the Well Tempered Clavier by J.S. Bach in Open Score
William Andrews

Contents

Section 1

Melody	1
Exercises	2
Tonal and modal degrees of the scale	6
Primary and secondary triads	6
Point-against-point (1/1)	7
Motion	8
Consonance	9
Perfect cadence structure	9
Analysis	9
Dissonance	10
Tritone	10
Sequence	12
Exercises	15
Analysis	18
Exercises	19

Section 2

Two-against-one rhythm (2/1)	24
Analysis	24
Exercises — sequences	31
Exercises	34
Three-against-one rhythm (3/1)	41
Analysis	42
Exercises — sequences	48
Exercises	50
Four-against-one rhythm (4/1)	58
Analysis	60
Exercises	64
Exercise — sequence	66
Exercises	67

Section 3

Miniature Compositions	78
Considerations	78
Open and closed cadences	81
Exercises	81
Exercises	84
Binary Compositions	86
Symmetrical	86
Asymmetrical	86
Analysis	88
Exercises	90
Rounded Binary Compositions	100
Analysis	101
Exercises	104
Ternary Compositions	113
Analysis	114
Exercises	116
Creation of Miniature Compositions	120
Exercises	120
Exercises	122

Section 4

Invertible Counterpoint	127
Analysis	129
Analysis — Fugue expositions	134
Exercises — inversion at the 8ve	139
Exercises — inversion at the 15th	141

Appendix Non-chord notes (tones)	146
Unaccented	146
Accented	146
Pedal point	147
Suspensions and syncopation	149
Exercises	149

Preface

Students of 18th century counterpoint should have a knowledge of the following:

i. Major and minor keys
ii. triads, chords of the 7th, including secondary dominants, secondary diminished 7ths
iii. cadences of all types
iv. modulation (with pivot chords)
v. non-chord notes of all types
vi. Binary and Ternary Forms with all their ramifications

A possible tempo should always be considered so that the flow and texture of the music may be felt.

The materials have been arranged so that the students are studying music from the great composers before attempting to write themselves. As a result of music being the text, as few rules as possible have been given.

A discussion of many items, such as canon, fugue, chorale prelude etc. will not be found here. Only those elements which are pertinent to an understanding of 18th century counterpoint and the working of the counterpoint examinations of the Royal Conservatory of Music have been included.

Circled numbers ((5)) refer to bar numbers.

For reference material one of the finest texts available "Counterpoint" 2nd edition, by K. Kennan, Prentice Hall 1972; is highly recommended.

We would like to thank our colleague, Maurice White, for permission to use his work on p. 144.

Above all, enjoy the music.

W. G. A. & M. L. S.

Section One
Melody

Study of contrapuntal music shows the importance of the melodic line of each voice. The single melodic line began naturally with the human voice. While instruments have a much wider range than the voice, their melodies spring from this vocal origin, and this singing quality must be retained.

The lyrical aspect of western tonal melody is further emphasized by being built on the triadic harmony (tertial system) of the common practice period. This type of melody contains movement by step and skip, showing clearly the chords on which it is constructed, and thereby outlining the tonality of the composition. The melodic span of these melodies is most often an 8ve, 9th or 10th; rarely do they extend beyond these intervals. Only in virtuosic coloratura melodies will these intervals be exceeded.

The shape or natural rise and fall (curve) of the melody is of paramount importance. Angularity is seldom a desirable feature. Any melodic skip of a 5th or more should turn back again before proceeding onwards.

After attempting to sing the following, offer a criticism of each.

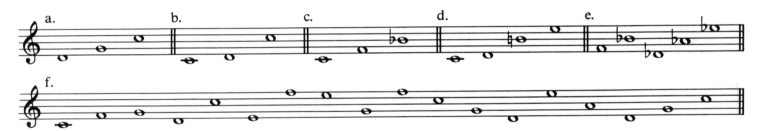

Augmented skips are only used for special effects, as in the following, and should otherwise be avoided.

Exercises

a. Sing the following melodies.
b. Plot the basic shape of each one, and state the span as shown in the worked examples.
c. Identify the non-chord notes.

Sonata

L. van Beethoven
Op. 10 No. 2

Presto

1.

F:

Basic
Shape

F: V   I
Span of basic shape ___one octave___

Sonata

W. A. Mozart
K. 331

Allegretto

2.

a: The appoggiatura is the only type of non-chord note in this melody.

a: I
Span of basic shape ___minor tenth___

Sonata for Flute

G. F. Handel

Allegro

3.

F:

F:

Span of basic shape _____

Messiah

G. F. Handel

Allegro
(Bass)

4.

C: Why   do   the   na - tions   so   fu - rious - ly   rage   to - ge - ther

Span of basic shape_____

Christmas Oratorio

Span of basic shape _____

Sonata

Span of basic shape _____

Sonata

Span of basic shape _____

Sonata

Span of basic shape _____

Christmas Oratorio

Span of basic shape _____

4

6

Tonal and Modal Degrees of the Scale

The tonal degrees are those which are common to a major scale and its tonic minor (natural form), that is the tonal degrees are I, II, IV, and V.

The modal degrees are those which are different in the two scales, that is III, VI, and VII.

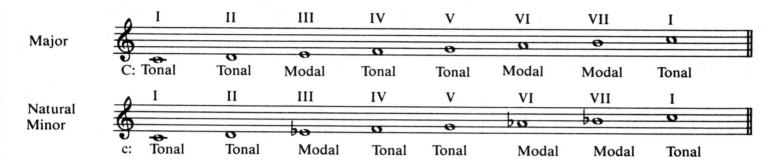

Write the tonal degrees in the following scales:

D major, e natural minor, f# natural minor, Ab major

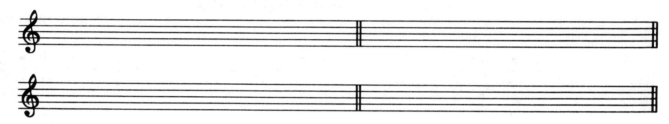

Primary and Secondary Triads

Primary triads in any key (major or minor) are those which have tonal degrees as the root and 5th, that is, I, IV, and V. The remaining triads are secondary triads, that is, II, III, VI, and VII.

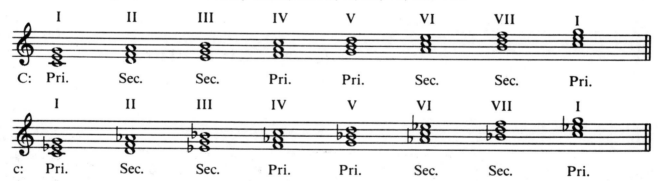

Write the primary triads in the following keys:

d natural minor, Eb major, g natural minor, B major

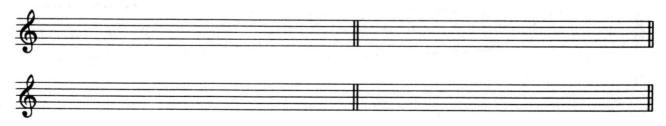

Point-Against-Point (1/1)

The Latin "punctus contra punctum" (point against point) shows the origin of the word counterpoint. It illustrates the idea of one note in one voice heard at the same time as one note in another voice. The combining of a melody in one voice with another melody in a second voice, both melodies having the same rhythm, results in the simplest form of counterpoint.

Consecutive (parallel) 4ths, 5ths, 8ves and unisons are found as part of the Mediaeval style, but do not occur in the Baroque and Classical styles.

Perform the following examples, listening to the interval qualities.

This uses parallel 4ths, 5ths and 8ves, moving in similar motion;

Parallel Organum

Musica enchiriadis (c. 850)

Principal Organum

Sit glo-ri-a Do-mi-ni, in sae-cu-la lae-ta-bi-tur Do-mi-nus in o-pe-ri-bus su-is

This uses 4ths, 5ths, 8ves, unisons and a few 3rds, moving chiefly in contrary motion;

Free Organum (12th century)
from Trope, Agnus Dei

pro - tho_____ plau_____ sti_____ sa_____ net_____ ut_____ a_____

_____ ctus:

Neither of these examples establish tonality or key as we know it.

8

In this Bach example the use of 3rds, 6ths and the tritone (augmented 4th, diminished 5th) establishes the tonality (key) of the music. These intervals are essential to the major-minor system with which we are familiar.

Motion

This example demonstrates the three fundamental types of motion:

1. Contrary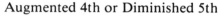

2. Similar

3. Oblique

Chorale

J. S. Bach
from Little Note Book
for Anna Magdalena Bach

The small notes confirm the chords which are implied by the melody and bass.

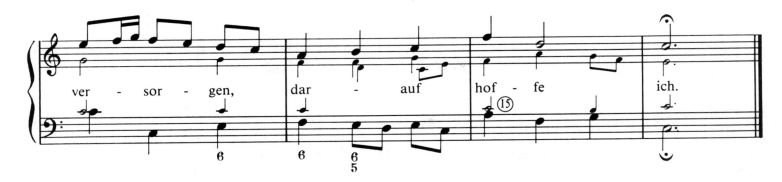

ver - sor - gen, dar - auf hof - fe ich.

In Baroque and Classical music consonance and dissonance were viewed as follows:

Consonance

a. The perfect consonances, which give a feeling of stability (p5, p8 and p1), are best at the end of a phrase. If used in the middle of a phrase, they should occur on a weak beat and be approached in contrary motion.

b. The imperfect consonances (3rd and 6th) are the ones that define the chord and may be used freely. The 3rd may be used as the last interval of any phrase except the final one.

c. The perfect 4th, which gives a feeling of instability, should only be used as a non-chord note, or when approached in contrary motion as part of the cadential $\frac{6}{4}$ chord.

Perfect Cadence Structure

Study the perfect cadence structure of examples a and b as analysed.

Variation No. 1, Suite X

G.F. Handel

a.

d: II⁶ V⁴ ─ 3 I _____

Minuet

L. Mozart

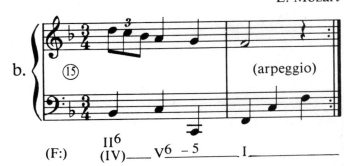

b.

(F:) II⁶ (IV) ── V⁶ – 5 I _____

Analysis

Analyse c to j similarly.

Minuet

T. A. Arne

c.

B♭:

Minuet

L. Mozart

d.

F:

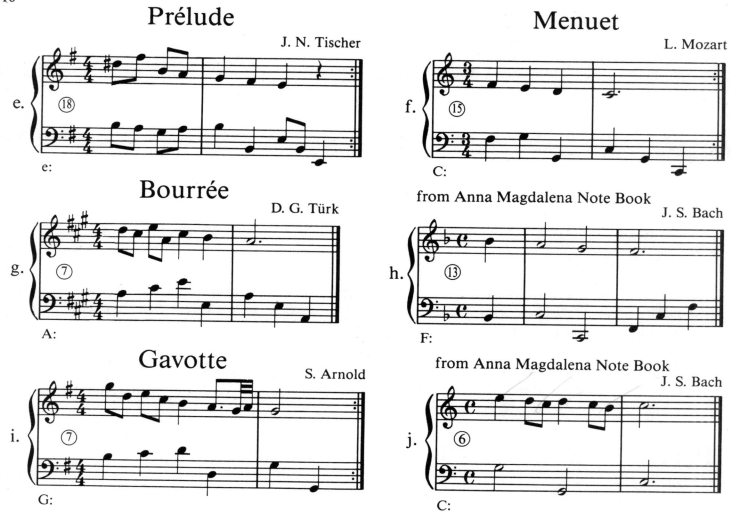

Prélude
J. N. Tischer

Menuet
L. Mozart

Bourrée
D. G. Türk

from Anna Magdalena Note Book
J. S. Bach

Gavotte
S. Arnold

from Anna Magdalena Note Book
J. S. Bach

Dissonance

a. The tritone (aug. 4th) or its inversion (dim. 5th) may be used, provided the aug. 4th moves outward to a 6th, or the dim 5th moves inward to a 3rd.

b. The 7th may be used provided the upper note resolves by a step to a 3rd.

c. The 2nd may be used provided the lower note resolves by a step to a 6th.

Tritone

Any tritone, as shown in 1a, may become two other tritones by means of enharmonic change. See 1b and 1c.

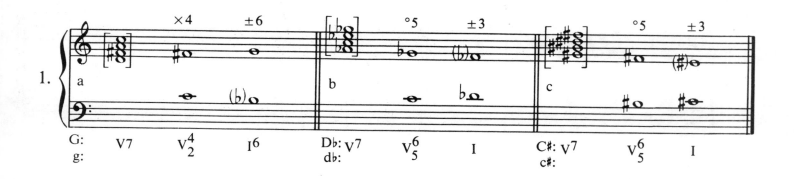

Complete and resolve the tritones in 2 to 6, showing keys, dominant 7ths and chord symbols as in number 1.

F A^{bb}C^bE^{bb}.   BDF

Sequence

The following chains of secondary dominants demonstrate the use of alternating intervals, as shown below, covering all keys (including rarely used enharmonic equivalents.) They all exhibit the cycle of 5ths, which in itself gives a sequential pattern, the root movement of which is in descending 5ths.

1. a & b: Alternating 3rds and 6ths.

The dotted lines clarify the root movement.

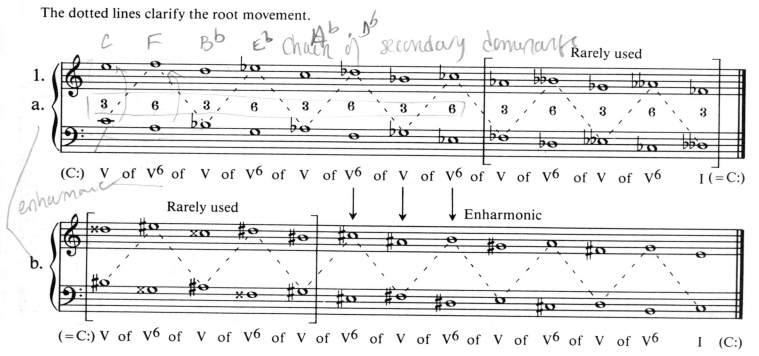

2. a & b: Alternating 6ths and 3rds.

The root movement is shown by the note names in each bar.

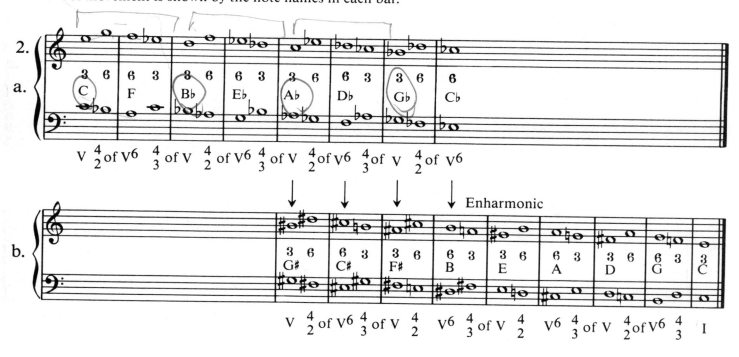

13

3. a & b: Alternating augmented 4ths and diminished 5ths.

This chromatic movement avoids false (cross) relation. The root movement is shown on the third staff.

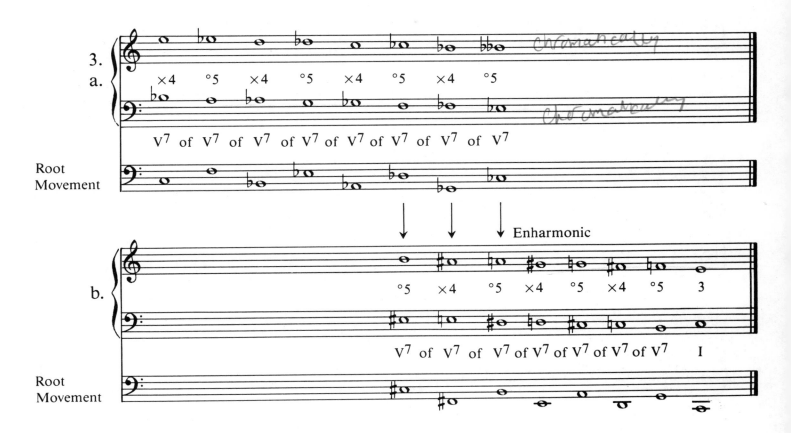

4. a & b: Alternating 3rds and 7ths.

The root movement is shown in the bass clef.

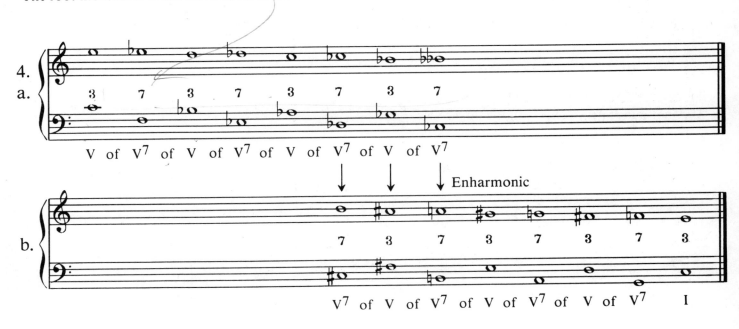

14

5. a & b: Alternating 7ths and 3rds.

The root movement is shown in the bass clef.

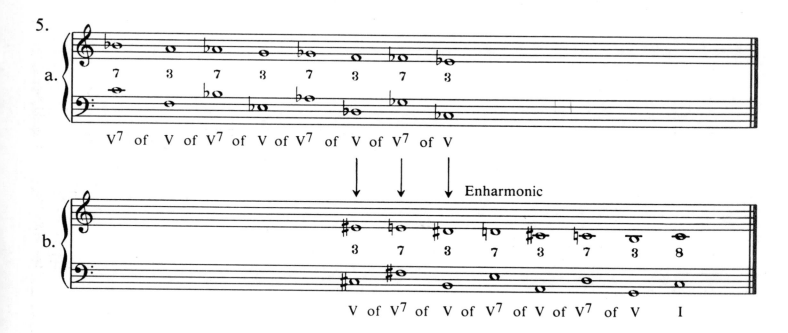

6. a & b: Alternating 2nds and 6ths.

The root movement is shown in the upper voice.

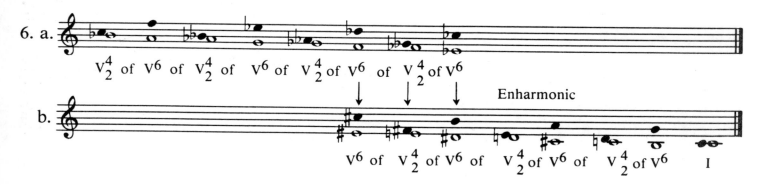

7. a & b: Alternating 6ths and 2nds.

The root movement is shown in the upper voice.

Exercises

The following passages show a similar sequential pattern, while *remaining within the key*. Passage 'b' is the inversion of 'a', as well as illustrating the sequence in the minor key. Note that the raised Leading Note is only used in the minor key to establish the final cadence.

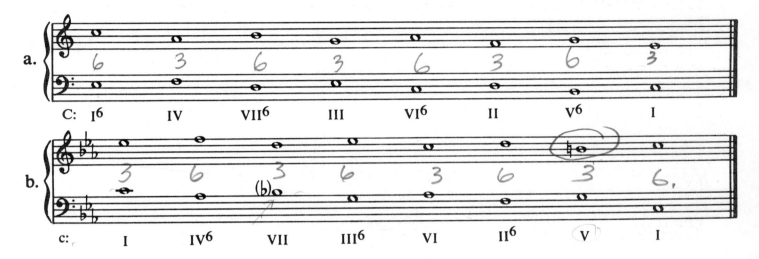

a. C: I^6 IV VII^6 III VI^6 II V^6 I

b. c: I IV^6 VII III^6 VI II^6 V   I

Write the sequence in 'a' in E major and A flat major.

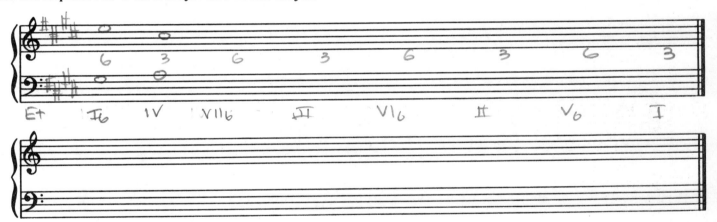

E+ I_6 IV VII_6 III VI_6 II V_6 I

Write the sequence in 'b' in f minor and e minor.

16

The following sequences represent the most frequently used *secondary dominants* of the tonal and modal degrees of the major and minor scales.

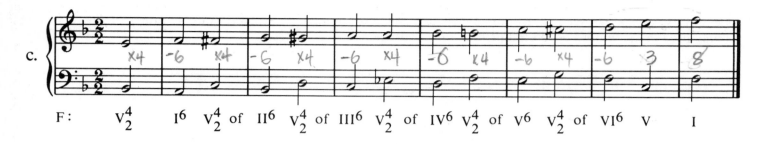

c.

F : V_2^4 I^6 V_2^4 of II^6 V_2^4 of III^6 V_2^4 of IV^6 V_2^4 of V^6 V_2^4 of VI^6 V   I

Write the sequence in 'c' in E flat major and D major.

d.

G :   V I^6 V of II^6 V of III^6 V of IV^6 V of V^6 V of VI^6 V   I

Write the sequence in 'd' in A major and B flat major.

d: V_2^4 I^6 V_2^4 of ♭VII⁶ V_2^4 of VI⁶ V_2^4 of V⁶ V_2^4 of IV⁶ V_2^4 of III⁶ V   I

Write the sequence in 'e' in g minor and a minor.

Write the sequence in 'f' in c sharp minor and f sharp minor.

b: V^6 I V^6 of ♭VII V^6 of VI V^6 of V V^6 of IV V^6 of III V^6 I

Analysis

Analyse the following compositions as examples of two-voice counterpoint in a one-against-one (1/1) rhythm. Symbolize the harmony and examine the intervals used between the voices. Observe the movement (shape and design) of the melodic line.

Give particular attention to the cadence structure.

Bourrée

Von Gott Will Ich Nicht Lassen

Herr Gott, Ich loben alle wir

from J. S. Bach

Bb: I   VI   III   IV

Exercises

a. Sing the given voice.
b. Add chord symbols where none are given.
c. Write the missing voice, paying particular attention to the VOCAL aspect of your LINE.

   Do not ignore the possibility of sequence, secondary dominants and modulation.

1.

Bb: I   I   V6   V   IV6   I   IV   V   I

2.

D: V6   I   IV6   V   I6   II7   V   I

20

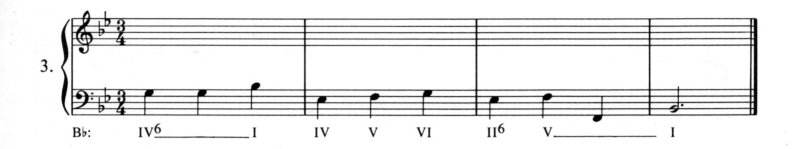

Bb: IV⁶_____I   IV   V   VI   II⁶   V_____I

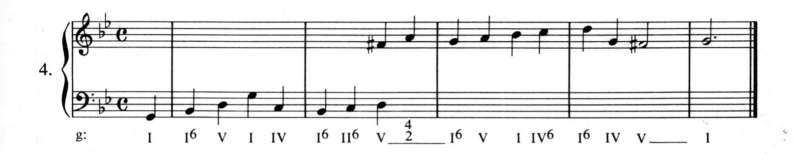

g: I   I⁶   V   I   IV   I⁶   II⁶   V___⁴₂___   I⁶   V   I   IV⁶   I⁶   IV   V____   I

from J. S. Bach

f: I   V⁶   V⁷   I   I⁶   V⁴___³___   I⁶   IV⁶   IV   V⁶___⁵___   I

d:

Chorale

D. Speer

G: I   I ——— V⁶   I   V⁶   I   V⁴₃ of V   IV   I ——— I

Liebster Immanuel, Herzog der Frommen

J. S. Bach

b: I   I   I⁶₄   V⁶   V⁷   I

Menuet

from G. F. Handel

9.

F: I   IV   I⁶   II   V⁷   I   IV   II   V

Menuet

from J. Krieger

10.

G:

Section Two
Two-Against-One Rhythm (2/1)

Perform passage 'a' and be aware of the use of consonant intervals, establishing harmonic clarity.

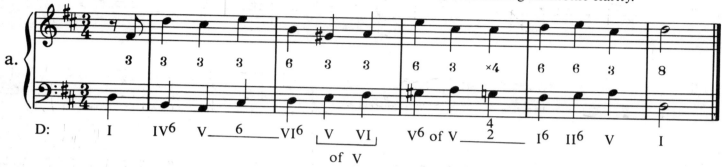

Perform passage 'b' with its added rhythmic movement. Notice the use of non-chord notes (tones) to decorate the basic melodic line.

Analysis

The movement of two notes-against-one (2/1) is only successful if the basic one-against-one is harmonically secure.

Complete the analysis of the following chorale, observing the rhythmic movement of the continuo bass, noting the use of sequence, auxiliary, passing and chord notes.

In the first four bars notice how the use of ⟦I⟧ ⟦IV⟧ ⟦V⟧ ⟦I⟧ clearly establishes the tonality.

O Gott, du frommer Gott

J. S. Bach

Continuo

Continue the analysis of the following Gavotte, observing the use of appoggiaturas, échappées and anticipations.

Students are reminded that the 7th of the V7 chord may be introduced as a decorating note, as in the opening. Notice in the second complete bar that the 7th of IV7 is transferred from the upper voice to the lower one which then proceeds to the resolution in bar 3.

Gavotte
Variation 3 (Suite XIV)

from G. F. Handel

Analyse the following compositions as examples of two-against-one (2/1) counterpoint. Symbolize the harmony; note the movement of the melodic line, the use of sequence and the resolution of all dissonances. Pay special attention to the intervals which form the basic 1/1 point.

Sarabande

A. Corelli

Key __

Prelude No. 2
(6 Little Preludes)

The circles indicating the note G in bars 29-31 show an implied dominant pedal; this is an essential point
in understanding the harmony of these bars.

J. S. Bach

Menuetto II

from Sonata in C: for Flute and Continuo

J. S. Bach

Exercises — sequences

Complete the following sequences, maintaining the 2/1 movement.

4. C   F   B♭   E♭

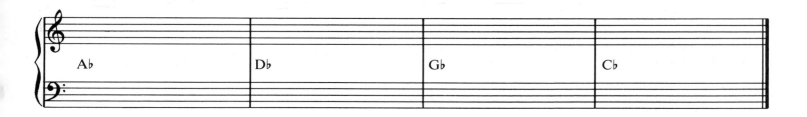

A♭   D♭   G♭   C♭

= ↓   Enharmonic

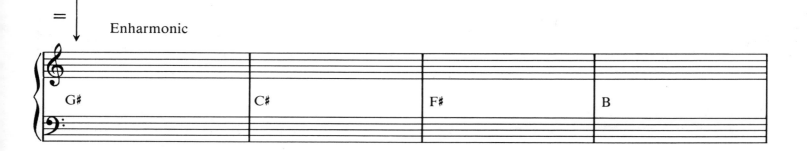

G#   C#   F#   B

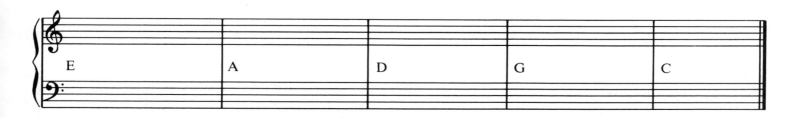

E   A   D   G   C

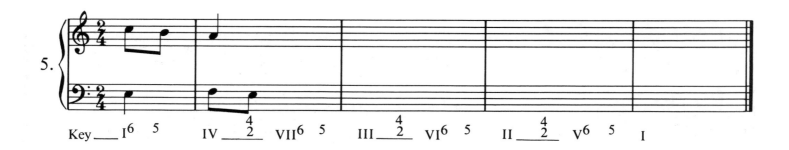

Key ___ I⁶ 5   IV ___ 4/2 VII⁶ 5   III ___ 4/2 VI⁶ 5   II ___ 4/2 V⁶ 5   I

These passages demonstrate unacceptable parallel 5ths, 7ths and 8ves.

Exercises

In writing 2/1 counterpoint, maintain a *vocal* style. Your melody must be singable, and have unity in design and obvious structure. You must observe sequence (melodic and harmonic) and maintain tonal clarity.

The skeletal structure and harmonic rhythm must be very clear, so as to support an elaborate line.

a. Symbolize the harmony.

b. In each exercise transform the note heads (which have no stems) into eighth notes, and add the second eighth note for each beat. The finished melody must be singable and have unity in design and obvious structure.

Key ___

Key ___

Key ___

Key ___

5. Key ___

6. Key ___

For the following:

a. Symbolize the harmony,
b. Continue the upper voice in quarter notes,
c. Circle and classify the non-chord notes.

from Cantata No. 133
"Ich freue mich in dir"

J. S. Bach

7.

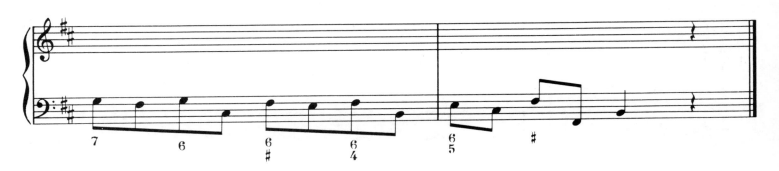

from Six Short Preludes No. 4

J. S. Bach

Aria

from J. Pachelbel

10.

a. Study bars 1-8 as analysed.

b. In bars 9-16:

  i. Symbolize the chords.

  ii. In the upper treble staff continue the decorative 2/1 movement according to the given figures and in a style similar to bars 1-8.

Canzonet

C. G. Neefe

11.

a. Symbolize the harmony.
b. Continue the missing bass in quarter notes, showing the 1/1 basis on which the moving continuo is built.

Nur freut euch, lieben Christen g'mèin,

J. S. Bach

Cont.

Key ___

Ich steh an dei - ner Krip - pen hier, o Je - su - lein, mein
Ich kom - me bring und schen - ke dir, was du mir hast ge -

Le - ben; Nimm hin, es ist mein Geist und Sinn, Herz,
ge - ben

Seel und Mut, nimm al - les hin, und laß dirs Wohl - ge - fal - len!

12.

a. Symbolize the harmony.
b. Observe in bars 1 and 2 how the continuous 8th note movement has been divided between the two voices.
c. Continue the upper voice so that there will be continuous 8th note movement throughout as illustrated in the opening. Use a half note at the end of each section where there is a half note in the lower voice.

Gavotte

from J. Krieger

Key ___

Three-Against-One Rhythm (3/1)

This is similar to 2/1 rhythm, but due to the faster motion, it needs more step-wise movement. Too many broken chords or arpeggio figures do not make a good melodic line.

Perform passage 'a' and be aware of the use of consonant intervals, establishing harmonic clarity.

from J. S. Bach

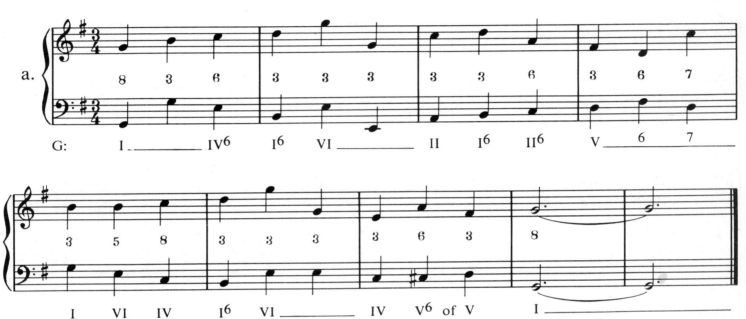

Perform passage 'b' with its added rhythmic movement. Notice the use of non-chord notes (tones) to decorate the basic melodic line. Observe the resolution of all dissonance.

J. S. Bach

The movement of three notes-against-one (3/1) is only successful if the basic one-against-one is harmonically correct.

Analysis

Complete the analysis of the following, observing the rhythmic movement of the oboe part, noting the use of sequence, non-chord notes and dissonances.

The first eight bars of the following have already been analysed in passages 'a' and 'b' on the previous page.

Continue the one-against-one reduction.

Jesu bleibet meine Freude
(from Cantata 147)

J. S. Bach

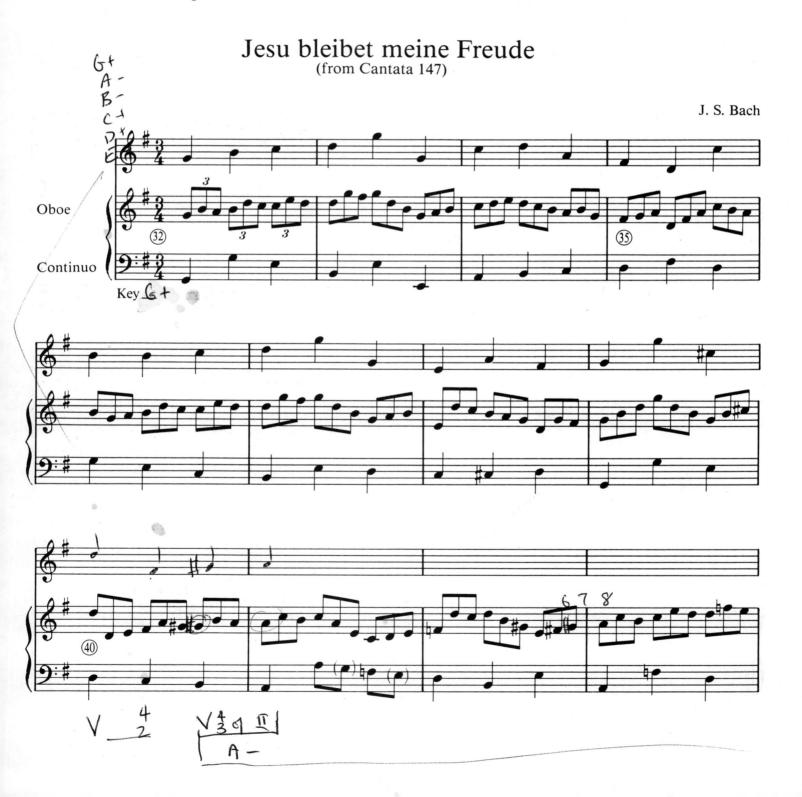

Analyse the following compositions as examples of three-against-one (3/1) counterpoint. Symbolize the harmony; note the movement of the melodic line, the use of sequence and the resolution of all dissonances. Pay special attention to the intervals forming the basic 1/1 point.

Observe the subdivision of ♩. into ♩ ♪

Gigue

J. S. Bach

from Symphony No. 9, Op. 125

(Last movement)

L. van Beethoven

Giga

D. Alberti

3.

Key ___

48

These passages demonstrate unacceptale parallel 5ths, 7ths and 8ves.

Exercises — sequences

Complete the following cycles of 5ths as begun.

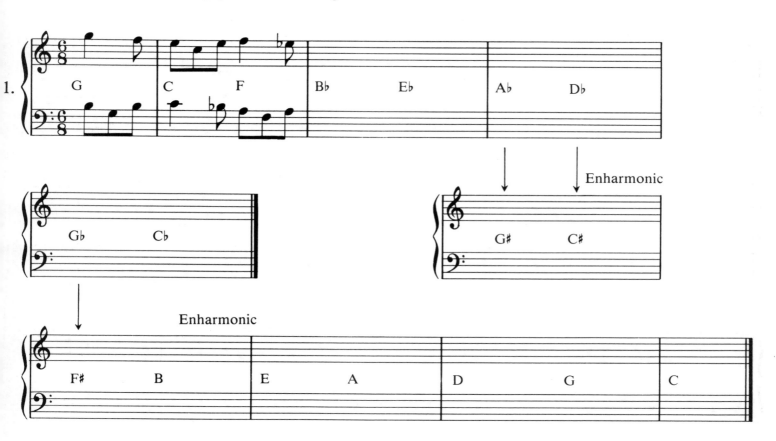

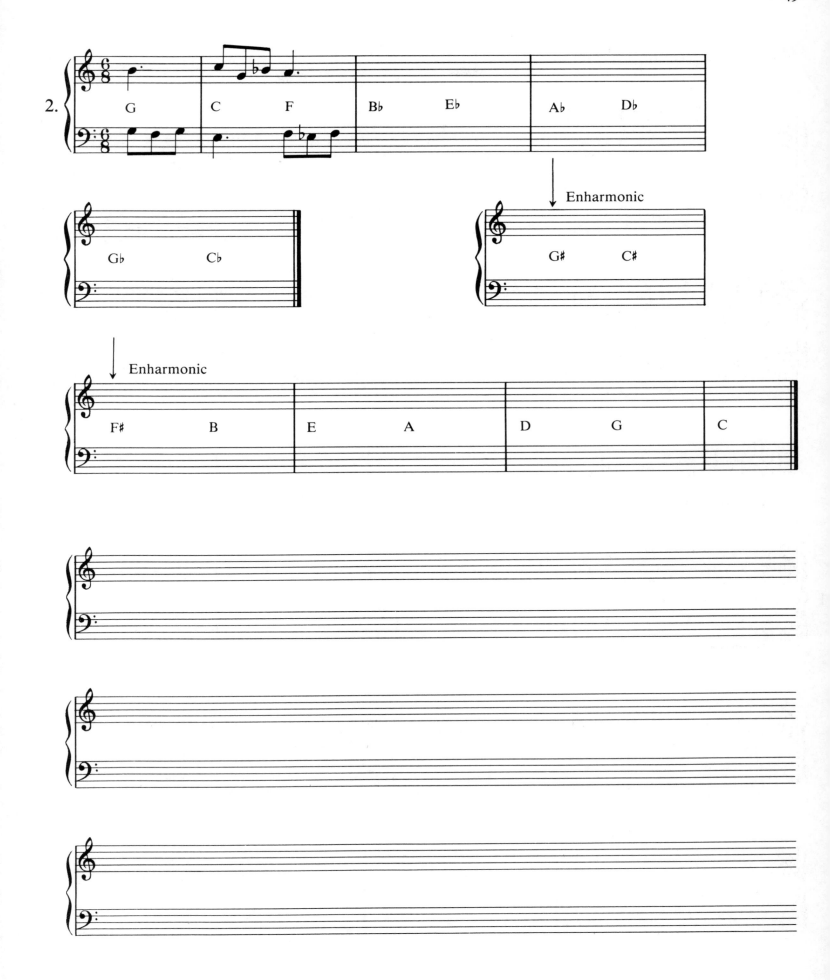

Exercises

For the following write a soprano in 3/1 rhythm. Show all chord symbols.

Key___

Key___

Key___

4. Key ____

5. Key ____

6. Key ____

51

7. Symbolize the implied harmonies of the following violin line. Write the continuo bass using ♩. and/or ♩♪.

Gigue

Allegro

C. P. E. Bach

Violin

Continuo

Key ____

Fine

Da Capo

8. Symbolize the following continuo line. Write an upper voice using ♩. and/or ♩ ♪ .

from Cantata No. 64
"Sehet, welch eine Liebe hat uns der Vater er zeiget."

J. S. Bach

9. Symbolize the following and continue the triplet 16th note movement.

from Cantata No. 32
"Liebster Jesu, mein Verlangen"

J.S. Bach

10. Complete the soprano in accordance with the figured bass.

from Cantata No. 159
"Sehet, wir geh'n hinauf gen Jerusalem"

J. S. Bach

from Cantata No. 51
"Jauchzet Gott in allen Landen"

J. S. Bach

11. Symbolize the harmony of the following. Write the missing voice, using rhythms similar to those suggested.

from Cantata No. 168
"Thue Rechnung! Donnerwort"

J. S. Bach

56

12.   Symbolize the harmony, and add the missing voice so that there will be continous 3/1 movement throughout.

Kommt, Seelen, dieser Tag

J. S. Bach

Key ___

Four-Against-One Rhythm (4/1)

As in 2/1 and 3/1 rhythm, the movement in 4/1 is only successful if the basic one-against-one is harmonically correct. The ornamentation, providing the rapid movement, should result in a smooth flowing melodic line.

Perform passage 'a' and be aware of the use of consonant intervals, establishing harmonic clarity and contrary motion. Note the use of the intervals of the 5th and 8ve at the beginning and end of the phrase. Complete the analysis as begun.

Chorale
"Alle Menschen müssen sterben"

Harmonization and variation from Pachelbel Organ Collection, Vol. IV.

J. Pachelbel

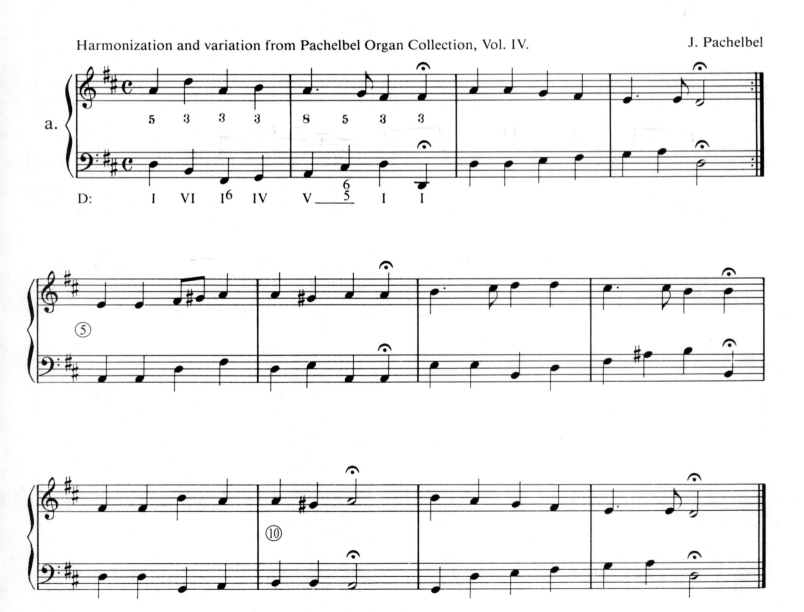

Perform passage 'b' with its added rhythmic movement. Notice the use of non-chord notes (tones) to decorate the basic melodic line. Observe the resolution of all dissonance. Complete the analysis as begun.

Variation (Partita) II

J. Pachelbel

Analysis

Analyse the following compositions as examples of four-against-one (4/1) counterpoint. Symbolize the harmony; note the movement of the melodic line, the use of sequence and the resolution of all dissonances. Pay special attention to the intervals forming the basic 1/1 point.

Prelude No. V
(W. T. C. Vol. I)

J. S. Bach

62

In the following example, observe that it is not a three-voice composition. The two upper lines are Bach's original, giving a 2/1 counterpoint. The lowest staff shows the basis of Bach's bass melody, and when combined with the top staff shows a 4/1 counterpoint.

Sei gegrüsset, Jesu gütig

(Partita diverse)

J. S. Bach

Herr Gott, Dich Loben Alle Wir

J. S. Bach

Observe the mixture of 4/1 and 2/1 counterpoint.

Exercises

Symbolize the following compositions. Complete the middle voice as begun, showing the basic 4/1 counterpoint.

Meinem Jesum Laß Ich Nicht

J. S. Bach

Mie - nem Je - sum   laß ich nicht,   geh ihm e - wig   an der Sei -

1.

Key __

ten; Chri - stus läßt mich für und für zu dem Le - bens - bäch - lein

lei - ten.   Se - lig,   der mit   mir so spricht: Mei - nem Je - sum   laß ich nicht.

from Variation Number III on a Chorale

F. X. A. Murschhauser

Key ___

66

Exercise — sequence

Complete the following cycle of 5ths as begun.

Enharmonic

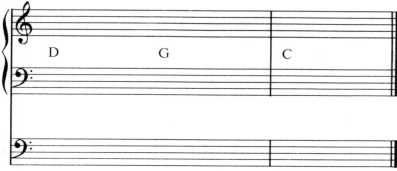

This passage demonstrates unacceptable parallel 5ths, 7ths, 8ves and 9ths.

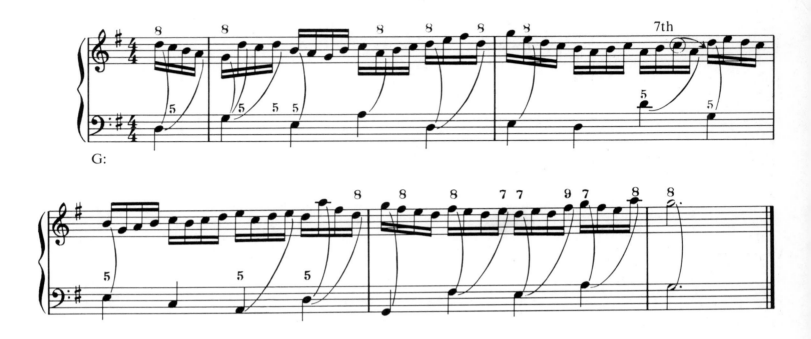

G:

Exercises

For the following write a soprano in 4/1 rhythm. Show all chord symbols.

1.

Key _____

68

2.

Key ____

3.

Key ____

4.

Key ____

5.

Key ____

Gavotte

from J. Pachelbel

6.

Key ____

IV / II

⑤

VI / I

J. Pachelbel

7.

Key ____

8. Complete the following as begun.

from Cantata No. 59
"Wer mich liebet, der wird mein Wort halten"

J. S. Bach

a.

Key ____

from Cantata No. 22
"Jesus nahm zu sich die Zwölfe"

J. S. Bach

Final Chorale

from Cantata No. 47
"Wer sich selbst erhöhet, der soll erniedriget werden"

J. S. Bach

9. Write a soprano in quarter notes. Show all chord symbols.

from Cantata No. 205
"Zerreisset, zersprenget, zertrümmert die Gruft"

J. S. Bach

10. Complete the following in the rhythm indicated. Show all chord symbols.

a.

1/1

Key ___

2/1

3/1

4/1

b.

1/1

Key____

Section Three
Miniature Compositions

Compositions on this scale may be categorized as:
 i. Binary
 ii. Ternary

Considerations

for the successful completion of these types are:

1. Harmonic clarity.
   Your study of the works in Section 2 demonstrate the absolute necessity of harmonic clarity and direction.

2. Melodic line and its embellishment.
   This is illustrated in Section 1 and the Appendix on page 146.
   Even though melodic line may be instrumental, it is essentially vocal in quality and style.

3. Motivic unity and sequence.
   A *motive* is a short melodic unit, used with sufficient frequency so as to provide musical unity. See the
   S. Arnold Gigue below. The motive is used with changing harmonies which conform to the binary form.

   Notice how the motive states the key and the rhythm, and the rhythmic unity of the cadences.

4. *Open* and *closed cadences* are explained on page 81.

Gigue

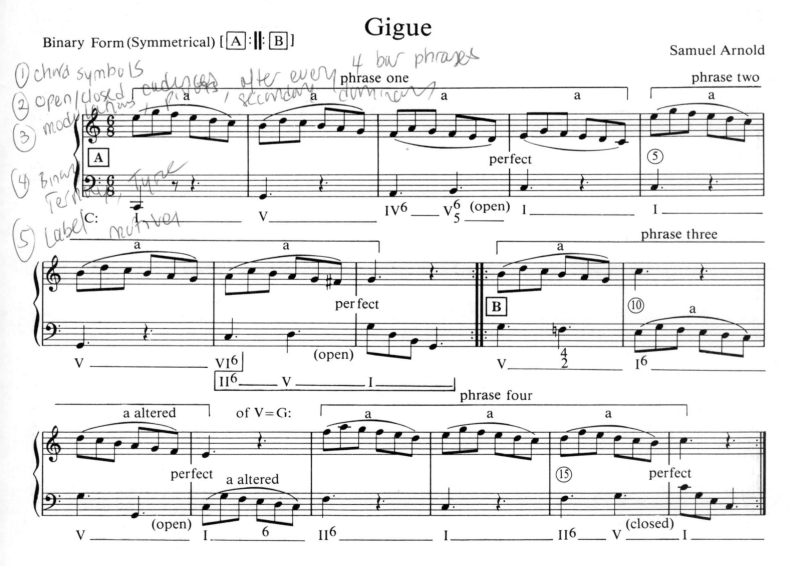

5. *Sequence* is identifiable as a transposed motive. Compare bars 11-12 with 9-10 of the W. F. Bach Menuett. Notice the cadential unity.

The motivic phrasing has been shown. The structural phrasing is 4 + 4 + 4 + 6 bars.

Menuett

W. F. Bach

6. *Imitation* (echo/canon)

Imitation is the echoing in the 2nd voice of the motive already announced in the 1st voice. This may occur with exact intervals, with tonal alteration of the intervals which provide clarity of key, or by inversion. The time interval may be from a few notes to several bars. While imitation may occur at any distance between the two voices, the most frequently used intervals are 4ths, 5ths, 8ves (simple or compound).

Allemande

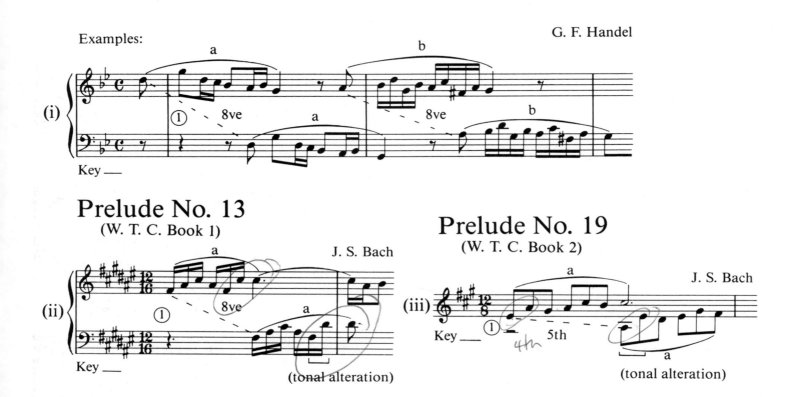

Prelude No. 13
(W. T. C. Book 1)

Prelude No. 19
(W. T. C. Book 2)

English Suite No. 1
Gigue

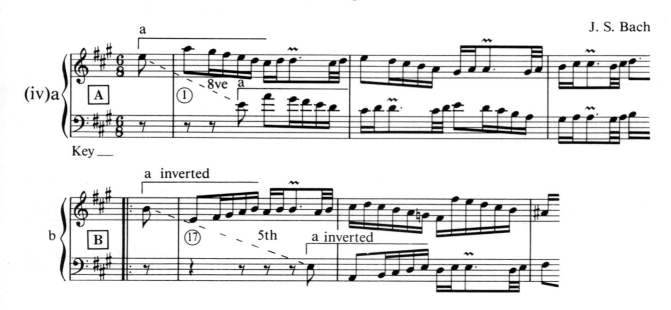

7. *Cadential strength*, (including 1st and 2nd endings).
   The cadences that establish the form are most satisfactory when both chords are in root position and divided by a bar-line. See Section 1, pages 9 and 10, and Section 3, pages 78 and 79.

8. ***Open*** and ***closed*** **cadences.**
   The *closed* cadence is V-I in the original key, with both chords in root position and the upper voice ending with Supertonic to Tonic or Leading Note to Tonic. V-I in the original key with one voice ending on the mediant is *semi-closed*. See examples 3 and 4. All other forms of perfect, imperfect or deceptive cadences are *open*.

Perfect

Imperfect

Deceptive

9. *Form and tonality.*
   The expected key changes will be discussed under each of the following: Binary, Ternary, and Rounded Binary forms.

Exercises

Mark the imitations (exact, altered or inverted) as shown on page 80. Identify the interval of imitation.

Bourrée

W. F. Bach

Key ___

Allemande from French Suite No. III

J. S. Bach

Duet for Two Hands

G. F. Handel

Ballett

J. P. Kirnberger

Jig

J. Clarke

Marche
(Anna Magdalena Book)

J. S. Bach

Key ___

Goldberg Variation No. 27

J. S. Bach

Canone alla Nona

Key ___

M. L. S.

Key ___

84

Exercises

For each of the following:

    i. Sing the given opening.
   ii. Add the missing voice in imitation of the given one.
  iii. Identify the interval of imitation.
   iv. State whether the imitation is *real* or *tonal*.

continue on given notes

Key ___

Key ___

Key ___

Key ___

Key ___

Key ___

Key ___

Binary Compositions
Symmetrical, Asymmetrical

Key Structure and phrase function

Binary Form is essentially four phrases. [A (4 + 4) :‖: B (4 + 4) or (4 + ?):‖]

See (i) S. Arnold Gigue page 78 (ii) W.F. Bach Menuett, page 79, and (iii) J.S. Bach Menuet, page 87.

Section A

This consists of 2 phrases (4+4)

The expected tonal direction in major keys is a move 'on' or 'in' the dominant before the double bar. 'On' the dominant is likely to be an imperfect cadence in the original key; 'in' the dominant indicates that the dominant chord is preceded by its own Leading Note, thereby making a perfect cadence in the dominant key. In the minor key the move will be 'on' or 'in' the dominant or relative major.

Phrase 1 must always establish the overall tonality of the composition. It will end melodically perfect open or imperfect open.

Phrase 2 achieves the modulation that establishes the form.

Section B

This also consists of 2 phrases (4+4) or (4+?)

This section often begins with the original motive in the new key. In preparing to close the composition, composers will often introduce extra bars, producing an *asymmetrical* composition. Short Binary compositions are usually *symmetrical* , but asymmetry is justifiable if the extra bars are needed in order to return to the tonic key. The return to the tonic key should be completed by the end of the third phrase or the beginning of the fourth.

Phrase 3 begins with the motive in its original form or in some form of inversion in the new key.

Phrase 4 must re-establish the original key, using material related to the original motive. If there is expansion to ? bars, it usually occurs in this phrase.

If the original motive is not used, material closely related as a type of development of the motive will be used.

1st endings satisfy the repeat signs and 2nd endings serve to complete the section.

Study the analysis, phrasing and structure, observing the very clear and simple harmonies, pivot chords, cadences, 1st and 2nd endings and the use of imitation linking phrases 3 and 4.

Further observe the abundance of contrary motion between the two voices.

Menuet
(Anna Magdalena Book)

The symbols under the bass line show primary harmonic direction and pivot areas. The symbols between the scores show secondary, passing or decorative harmonies.

Analysis

Study and analyse the following in the manner of the foregoing J. S. Bach

Menuett

Form _____

L. Mozart
From the Notebook for N. Mozart

1.

Key ____

Minuetto

Form _____

A. Corelli

2.

Key ____

Praeludium

J. C. F. Bach

Form _____

Key ____

Exercises

Using the models already given, complete the following compositions, achieving as tight a musical structure as possible. Plan the motivic unity very carefully.

Bourrée
from Flute Sonata No. 5

from G. F. Handel

Menuet

W. A. Mozart

Menuetto

Form _____

J. C. F. Bach

Minuet

Form _____

L. Mozart

92

March

M. L. S.

5.

Key ___

Bourrée

M. L. S.

6.

Key ___

Duet for Two Violas

W. F. Bach

Form _____

7.

Key ___

Giga

M. L. S.

8.

Key ___

Menuet

Form _____

J. C. F. Bach

Key ___

Bourrée

Form _____

from J. Krieger

Key ___

Pièce

Form _____

M. L. S.

11.

Key ___

Arioso

A. Scarlatti

12.

Key ___

Air

G. F. Handel

Form _____

Key ____

Minuetto

G. P. Telemann

Form _____

Key ___

98

Menuet

Form _____

J. Kuhnau

15.

Key _____

Minuet
from French Suite No. 4

J. S. Bach

Form _____

Key _____

Rounded Binary Compositions

This differs from Binary (Symmetrical and Asymmetrical) only in the final phrase(s). All key structures and phrase functions remain the same. In phrase 4, instead of material related to the original motive, there is a direct quote of the opening of the composition. This re-statement will always be altered to achieve a perfect cadence in the tonic key. This type of Binary is found in both symmetrical and asymmetrical structures.

Study the analysis, phrasing and structure of this Minuet by H. Purcell, observing the harmonies, pivot chords and the use of melodic material.

Minuett

Rounded Binary Form [A :‖ B   A]

H. Purcell

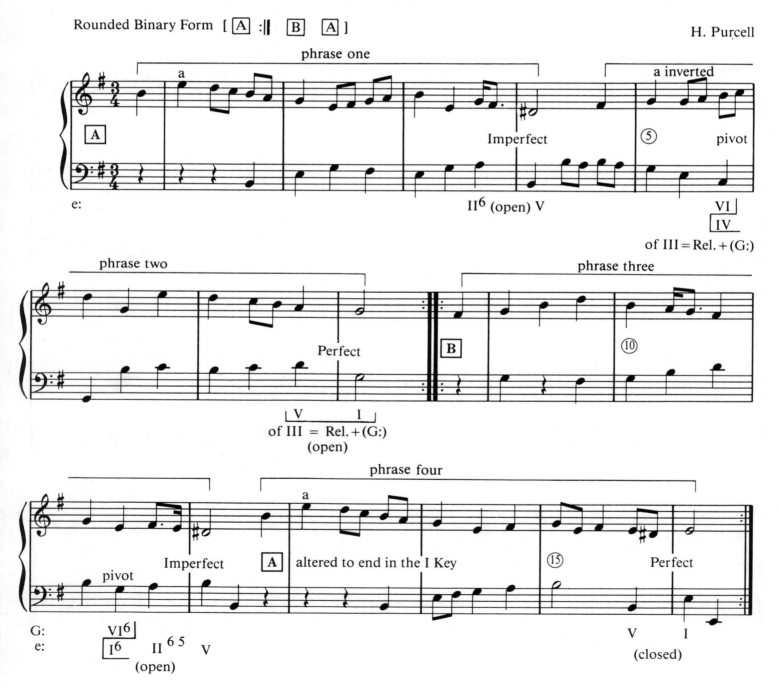

Analysis

Complete an analysis of the following in the manner of the foregoing Purcell Minuet.

Menuett

Form _____

W. A. Mozart

Key ____

Gigue

Form _____

M. L. S.

Key _____

Partita
Prélude

J. N. Tischer

Form _____

3.

Key ___

Exercises

Using your study of the preceding models, complete the following compositions by planning (a) the tonal structure, (b) the phrasing and (c) the form and (d) the use of material already given (motive, sequence, imitation).

Menuet

G. Böhm

Form _____

Key ___

Minuet

G. P. Telemann

Form _____

2.

Key ____

106

Minuet

Form _____

G. P. Telemann

Menuett

Form _____

G. P. Telemann

Key ___

Andante
(Septet, Op. 20)

Form _____

from L. van Beethoven

Piano Concerto in F

from W. A. Mozart

Form_____

Key ___

Duet for Two Violas

Form _____

W. F. Bach

7.

Key ____

Allegretto

M. L. S.

8.

Key ____

Pièce d'Imitation

Form_____

from G. P. Telemann

Key_____

Ternary Compositions

Key structure and phrase function

Ternary Form is essentially 6 phrases. A (4 + 4) B (4 + 4) A (4 + 4)

Section A

This consists of 2 phrases (4+4)

Phrase 1 establishes the tonality and usually ends with an imperfect (open) cadence.

Phrase 2 continues the melodic idea, and ends with a perfect (closed) cadence in the tonic key.

Section B

This also consists of 2 phrases (4+4), which always provide key contrast and often have melodic contrast.

In major compositions the key contrast is usually the dominant or relative minor. In minor compositions the key contrast is almost invariably the relative major.

Phrase 3 establishes the key of this section and ends with an open cadence.

Phrase 4 continues the melodic idea and ends with a closed cadence in the key of Section B .

One of the voices (usually the bass) will prepare tonally for the return of Section A .

Section A is achieved by D. C. (Da Capo), or it may be written out with variation.

The following compositions by L. Mozart and G. F. Handel demonstrate the foregoing.

Entrée

Ternary Form [A :‖: B :‖ A ‖]

L. Mozart

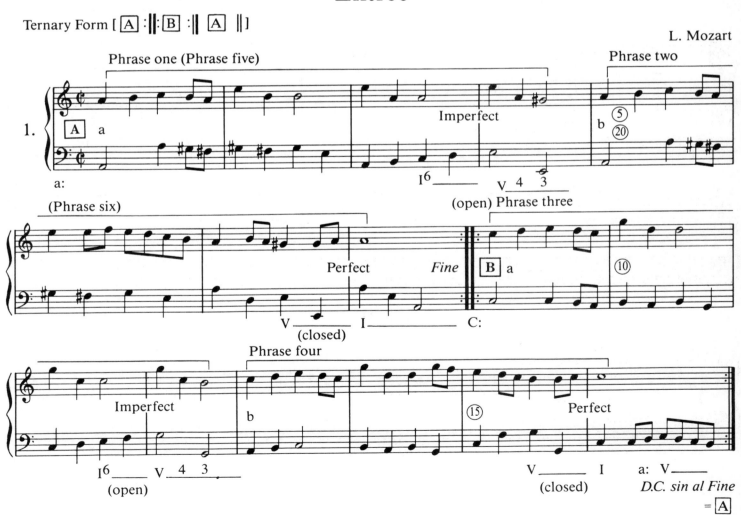

Menuett

Analysis

Study and analyse the following in the manner of the foregoing compositions.

Menuet

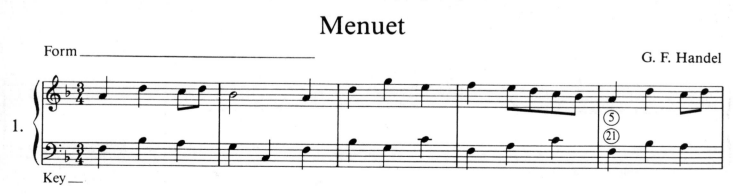

Minuet

Form _____

J. P. Rameau

2.

Key ___

Exercises

Using your study of the preceding models, complete the following compositions by planning (a) the tonal structure, (b) the phrasing and (c) the form and use of material already given (motive, sequence, imitation).

Minuet

Form _____

J. Clarke

Key ___

Menuett

Form _____

J. S. Bach

Key ___

117

Creation of Miniature Compositions

These three composition formats show an architectural structure that works well for most students. Consider the possibility of first and second endings in many of your compositions as in the J. S. Bach Menuet on page 87. Always write the cadences and plan the beginning of section B. Remember that the return of the opening in bar 13 will make a very satisfactory Rounded Binary form.

Do NOT experiment with irregular (asymmetrical) structures until you are very comfortable with the symmetrical types.

Exercises

Complete the three Gigues that follow. Notice the use of *inversions* and of *cadential unity*. They are all symmetrical Binary form.

Gigue

Gigue

Exercises

i. Select an opening and choose a suitable tempo.

ii. Sing the two voices several times to develop a feeling for the lines and their rhythmic flow.

iii. Set up the barline structure for **Binary** or **Ternary** (your choice). See pages 86, 100, 113, 120-121

iv. Plan the tonal structure to complement the chosen form.

v. Set up the cadence structure.

vi. Explore (on rough paper) some of the possibilities of developing the given opening (inversion, modulation, etc.).

vii. Complete the composition, aiming for cadential unity, symmetry, balance by sufficient use of the motive and overall musicality.

1.

Key __

from J.S. Bach

2.

Key __

J. S. Bach

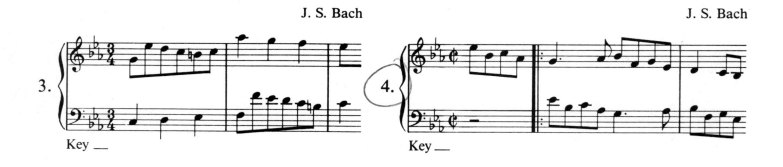

3.

Key __

J. S. Bach

4.

Key __

J. S. Bach

5.

Key __

F. W. Zachau

6.

Key__

124

17.   Key ___

20.   Key ___

21.   Key ___

22.   Key ___

23.   Key ___

24.   Key ___

25.   Key ___

26.   Key ___

27.   Key ___

28.   Key ___

Section Four
Invertible Counterpoint

When two contrapuntal voices are written in such a way that either voice will make a good bass for the other, this is called invertible counterpoint or double counterpoint. Invertible counterpoint may be written so that it will invert at the 15th (two 8ves), 8ve, 10th or 12th.

The two voices in double counterpoint may be rhythmically contrasting, or may be imitative.

The following fragments demonstrate imitation, inversion and rhythmic contrast.

Note the absence of parallel perfect 4ths, which when inverted would become parallel perfect 5ths.

AVOID THEM !

Prelude No. XX
(W. T. C. Vol. II)

J. S. Bach

128

Fugue XV
(W. T. C. Vol. I)

J. S. Bach

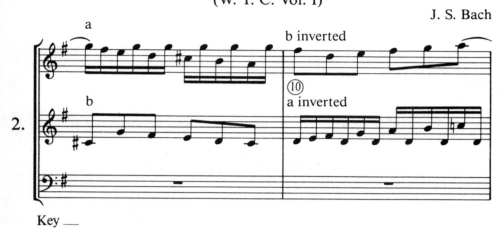

Key —

Prelude No. 2,
(W. T. C. Vol. II)

J. S. Bach

Key —

Pasacaille

G. F. Handel

Key —

Analysis

Analyse the following in the manner of the foregoing.

Trio

Beethoven
Op. 2, No. 1

1.

Key ___

Invention VI

J. S. Bach

Key _____

132

Fugue X
(W. T. C. Vol. I)

What is the relationship of:

i. bars 5-10 to bars 24-29?

ii. bars 15-18 to bars 34-37?

J. S. Bach

Analysis

The following fugal expositions (the first part of a fugue) all contain invertible counterpoint; analyse them by marking the main motive (subject) and the countermotive (countersubject). Observe the relative positions of subject and countersubject, and state whether the inversion is at the 8ve, 10th, 12th or 15th.

Fuga XII
(W. T. C. Vol. I) a 4 Voci
J. S. Bach

Fuga XVI
(W. T. C. Vol. I) a 4 Voci
J. S. Bach

136

Fuga XXIV
(W. T. C. Vol. I) a 4 Voci

J. S. Bach

Fuga VIII
(W. T. C. Vol. II) a 4 Voci

J. S. Bach

Fuga XX
(W. T. C. Vol. I) a 4 Voci

J. S. Bach

Fuga XVII
(W. T. C. Vol. II) a 4 Voci

J. S. Bach

Fuga XVI
(W. T. C. Vol. II) a 4 Voci

J. S. Bach

Key ___

Exercises — inversion at the 8ve.

Work the following in invertible counterpoint at the 8ve.

from G. F. Handel

1.

Key ___

from J. S. Bach

2.

Key ___

from J. S. Bach

3.

Key ___

from J. S. Bach

4.

Key __

from J. S. Bach

5.

Key __

from J. S. Bach

6.

Key __

Exercises — inversion at the 15th

Work the following in invertible counterpoint at the 15th.

142

from J. S. Bach

6.

Key ___

V of V

G. F. Handel

7.

Key ___

M. L. S.

8.

Key ___

from G. F. Handel

9.

Key ___

Mass in B Minor
Confiteor unum baptisma

J. S. Bach

10.

D: A — men, A —

— men, A —

— men, ven-tu-ri Sae-cu-li, A — men

M. White

11.

Key ___

Work no. 12 at the 8ve.

M. L. S.

12.

Key ___

Appendix Non-chord notes (tones)

1. Unaccented:

Observe that the 1st note of the beat is a CONSONANCE.
The 2nd note of the beat may be:

   i. *Passing note (tone)*

   ii. *Auxiliary note (neighbour tone):*

   iii. *Anticipation:* This is best at an ending, in the soprano only.

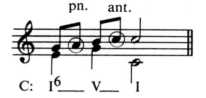

   iv. *Echappée:*

   v. *Another chord note:*

2. Accented:

The consonance may be displaced by an *appoggiatura*,
which moves downwards to the chord note.

The appoggiatura may move up, only if (a) it moves a half tone
OR (b) the 6th of the scale moves up to the 7th.

3. Pedal Point

Prelude No. 1
(W. T. C. Vol. II)

J. S. Bach

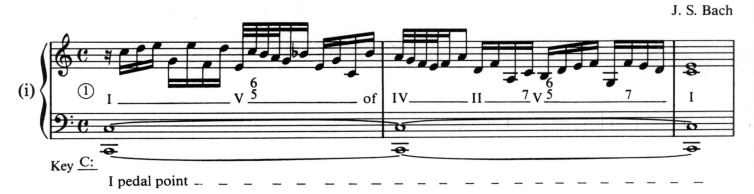

(i)

① I _____ V $\frac{6}{5}$ _____ of IV _____ II _____ 7 V $\frac{6}{5}$ _____ 7 _____ I

Key C:

I pedal point _ _ _ _ _ _ _ _ _ _ _ _ _ _ _ _

Complete the analysis of (ii) to (vii) in the style of (i) above.

Fugue VII
(W. T. C. Vol. I)

J. S. Bach

(ii)

③⑦

Key ___

Preludio II
(18 Little Preludes and Fugues)

J. S. Bach

(iii)

Key ___

⑤

Preludio X
(18 Little Preludes and Fugues)

J. S. Bach

Preludio XVII
(18 Little Preludes and Fugues)

J. S. Bach

Prelude No. VI
(W. T. C. Vol. I)

J. S. Bach

Preludio IV
(18 Little Preludes and Fugues)

J. S. Bach

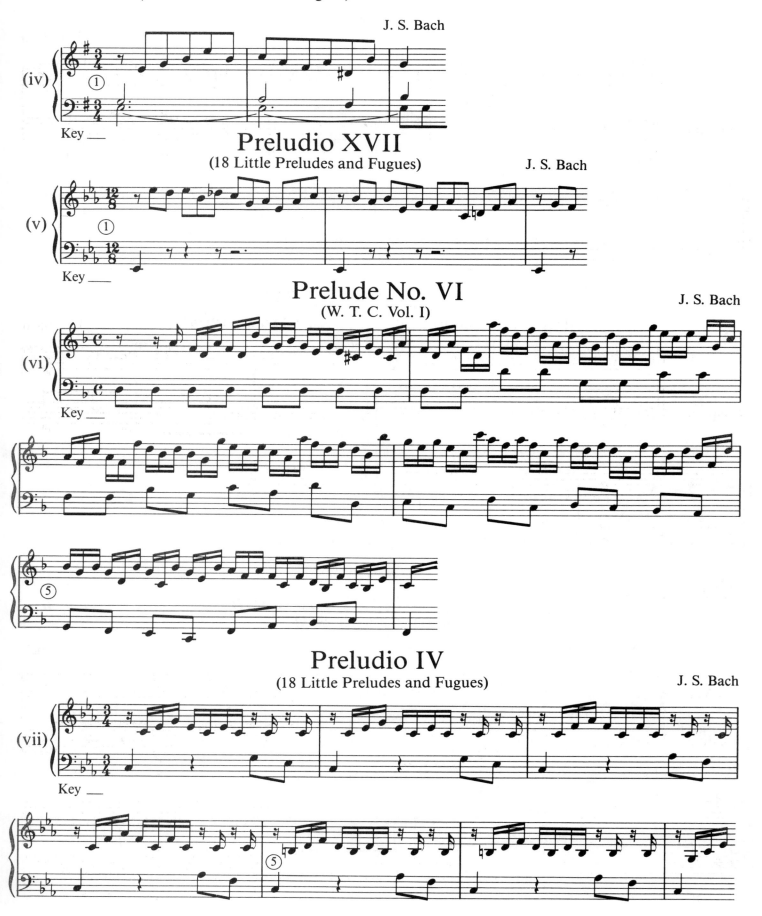

4. Suspensions and syncopation.

Continue marking the intervals of the syncopations and suspensions as begun.

from Cantata No. 30
"Freue dich, erlöste Schar"

J. S. Bach

from Cantata No. 213
Dramma per Musica "Laßt uns sorgen, laßt uns wachen"

J. S. Bach

Exercises

from Weihnachts Oratorium
(Christmas Oratorio) Part II

1. Complete the soprano according to the given numbers.

J. S. Bach

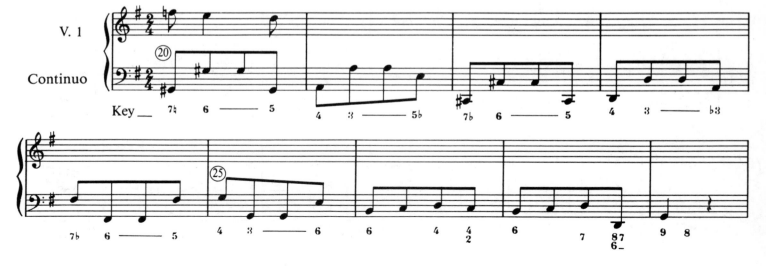

2. Complete the interval **analysis** between the two upper voices, as begun in bar 44.

from Cantata No. 4
"Christ lag in Todesbanden"

J. S. Bach